Library of
Davidson College

Japanese Capital Exports: Trends and Implications for the LDCs

**Office of Trade and Investment Analysis
International Trade Administration
U.S. Department of Commerce**

Japanese Capital Exports: Trends and Implications for the LDCs

Office of Trade and Investment Analysis
International Trade Administration
U.S. Department of Commerce

332.6
D781j

ISBN: 0-87186-340-5 (paperback)

First printing in bound-book form: 1988
First printed in the United States of America

PRICE: $3.50

89-12155

COMMITTEE FOR ECONOMIC DEVELOPMENT
477 Madison Avenue, New York, N.Y. 10022 / (212) 688-2063
1700 K Street, N.W., Washington, D.C. 20006 / (202) 296-5860

CONTENTS

TEXT

Introduction..1

Part One: Japanese Capital Exports............................2

    The Japanese Capital Account..............................2

    Long-Term Capital Flows...................................4

    Comparison of Japanese Capital Flows to Those of Other Industrial Nations..7

    The Concentration of Japanese Investment in the United States...9

    Japanese Capital Flows in First Half of 1987..............11

Part Two: The Role of Japanese Capital Exports in LDCs........12

    The Flow of Financial Resources to Developing Countries....12

    Japanese Position on the Debt Crisis......................14

    Recent Initiatives by the Government......................15

    The Future Role of Japanese Capital in LDCs...............16

TEXT TABLES

Table 1: Japanese Capital Account.............................4

Table 2: Composition of Japan's Long-Term Capital Flows.......5

Table 3: Japanese Overseas Direct Investment by Country.......7

Table 4: Japanese Overseas Direct Investment by Sector and Region...................................8

Table 5: Japanese Overseas Direct Investment in Commerce and Services................................9

Table 6: Stock of Overseas Direct Investment: Selected Countries......................................9

Table 7: Japanese Long-Term Net Capital Outflows by Region...11

Table 8: Official Japanese Flows to Developing Countries and Multilateral Agencies..............................13

Table 9: Exposure of Japanese and U.S. Banks to Selected Nations.......................................14

TEXT FIGURES

Figure 1:   Japan's Net External Assets............................2
Figure 2:   Japan's Current and Capital Accounts..................2
Figure 3:   Japanese Net Long-Term Capital Flows..................3
Figure 4:   Composition of Net Capital Flows.....................4
Figure 5:   Overseas Direct Investment as Percentage of GNP......10
Figure 6:   Overseas Direct Investment per Capita................10
Figure 7:   Flow of Financial Resources to Developing
            Countries from Japan and DAC Countries...............12

FOREWORD

This paper, Japanese Capital Exports: Trends and Implications for the LDCs, was researched and written by Anne M. Driscoll of the U.S. Department of Commerce.

The Committee for Economic Development (CED) is publishing this paper as a public service to make it available to those working on issues relevant to U.S.-Japan economic relations. This paper is an analytical document and should not be construed as a statement of U.S. Department of Commerce or CED policy.

CED is an independent, nonprofit, and nonpartisan organization comprised of 250 corporate and academic leaders. Our members actively develop policy analysis and recommendations by blending their practical experience and background knowledge with the research capabilities of expert economists and social scientists.

CED, in collaboration with its Japanese counterpart organization, Keizai Doyukai (the Japan Association of Corporate Executives), has been studying various aspects of U.S.-Japanese economic relations for a number of years. The latest joint project of the two organizations is developing a semi-annual bulletin on U.S. and Japanese trade and economic developments.

Additional copies of the following paper can be ordered from CED in New York at (212) 688-2063. Questions on the content of the paper should be directed to Anne M. Driscoll at (202) 377-3913.

Robert C. Holland
President
Committee for Economic Development

INTRODUCTION

In the past two years, as a result of its large and sustained current account surpluses--$49 billion in 1985, $86 billion in 1986 and a projected $85 billion in 1987--Japan has emerged as the world's number one capital exporter. Net capital outflows from Japan are likely to remain significant even as its trade surplus declines because rising income from its growing stock of overseas holdings will offset decreases in the merchandise trade component of the current account. The large current account surpluses have attracted increasing attention to the role of Japanese capital in the world economy. There is growing sentiment--especially in the United States--that Japan should take a larger financial role in the third world, using its excess capital to ease short-term debt-servicing difficulties and to promote long-term economic development in troubled third-world economies.

This paper examines Japanese capital exports. It is divided into two parts. The first examines recent trends in Japanese investment, presenting statistical data on capital flows and discussing changes in Japanese direct and portfolio investment abroad. The second part looks at Japan's role in the LDCs, focusing particular attention on the recently undertaken Japanese initiative to recycle $30 billion of its current account surpluses into the developing world.

PART ONE: JAPANESE CAPITAL EXPORTS

THE JAPANESE CAPITAL ACCOUNT

In 1985, Japan emerged as the world's leading creditor nation. Its net external assets--$129.8 billion at end of year 1985 and $180 billion in 1986--have increased significantly since 1981 when Japan's net external assets were $10.9 billion and the private sector had net external liabilities of $18.5 billion (figure 1). The growth of its large current account surpluses--which by definition must be matched by corresponding capital outflows (figure 2) and changes in its net claims on foreigners--has resulted in dramatic increases in Japanese investment abroad.

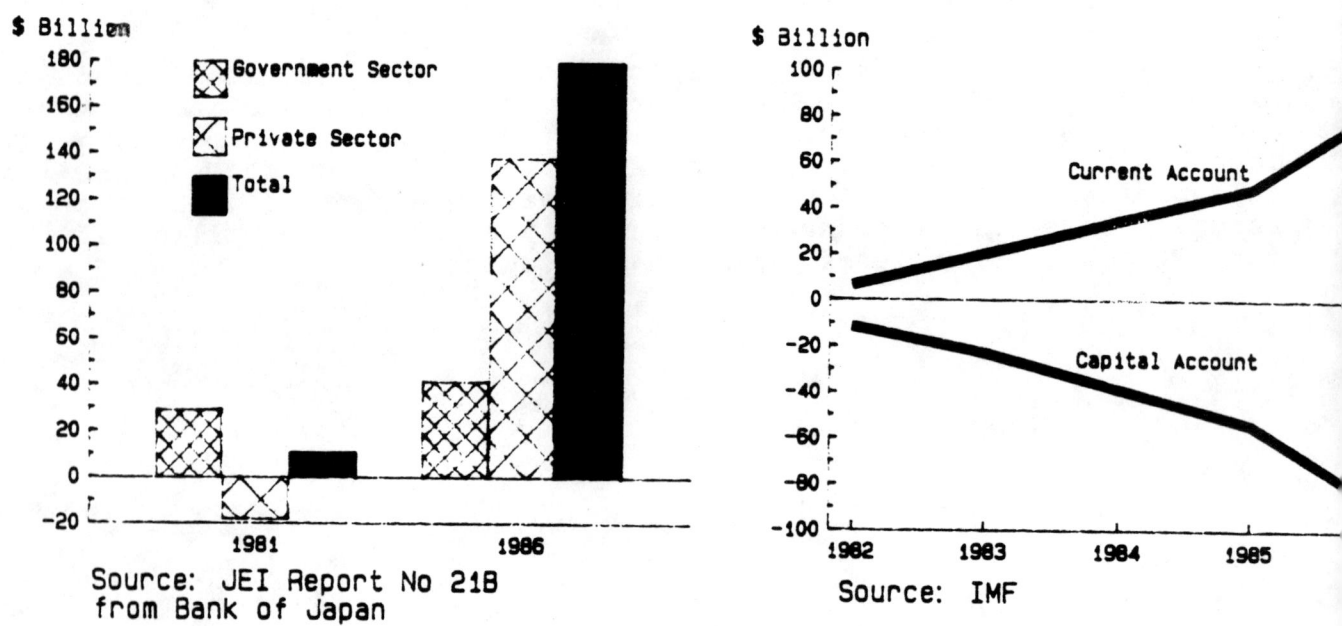

Figure 1

Japan's Net External Assets
1981, 1986

Source: JEI Report No 21B
from Bank of Japan

Figure 2

Japan's Current and Capital Account
1982-1986

Source: IMF

The capital account contains four principal types of transactions.

Direct investment--the establishment or purchase by residents of one country of a substantial ownership and management share of a business enterprise or real property in another country, or an increase in the amount of existing investment.

-a substantial ownership means at least 10 percent of the voting stock or equivalent interest.

Portfolio investment--international transactions in securities with an original term to maturity greater than one year.

Other long-term capital flows--drawings on or repayments of loans extended or any other long term transaction that does not fall into the portfolio or direct investment categories.

Short-term capital flows--international transactions in securities with an original term to maturity of less than one year, and international shifts in the control of liquid funds.

There have been significant changes in Japan's capital account transactions in the last several years (table 1). Net capital flows attributable to portfolio investments soared from a slight inflow of funds in 1982 to a huge net outflow of $102 billion in 1986 (figure 3), and net direct investment abroad increased by $10 billion to $14 billion in 1986. The 1986 direct and portfolio investments outflows were more than double the 1985 figures. At the same time, net short-term capital inflows increased dramatically from $9.7 billion in 1985 to $58.9 billion in 1986 as Japanese banks borrowed short-term in international capital markets to help finance long-term investments overseas (figure 4).

Table 1

Japanese Capital Flows*
(Billions of Dollars)

	1982	1983	1984	1985	1986
Capital Account, total	-11.33	-22.59	-38.40	-53.82	-89.05
of which:					
Direct Investment	-4.10	-3.20	-5.97	-5.81	-14.25
Portfolio Investment	0.84	-2.90	-23.96	-41.75	-102.18
Other Long-Term Capital	-12.99	-12.63	-20.08	-15.70	-16.00
Short-Term Capital	0.05	-2.59	13.44	9.73	58.92
Total Changes in Reserves	4.87	-1.27	-1.83	-0.29	-15.54

*minus sign indicates outflow
Source: IMF

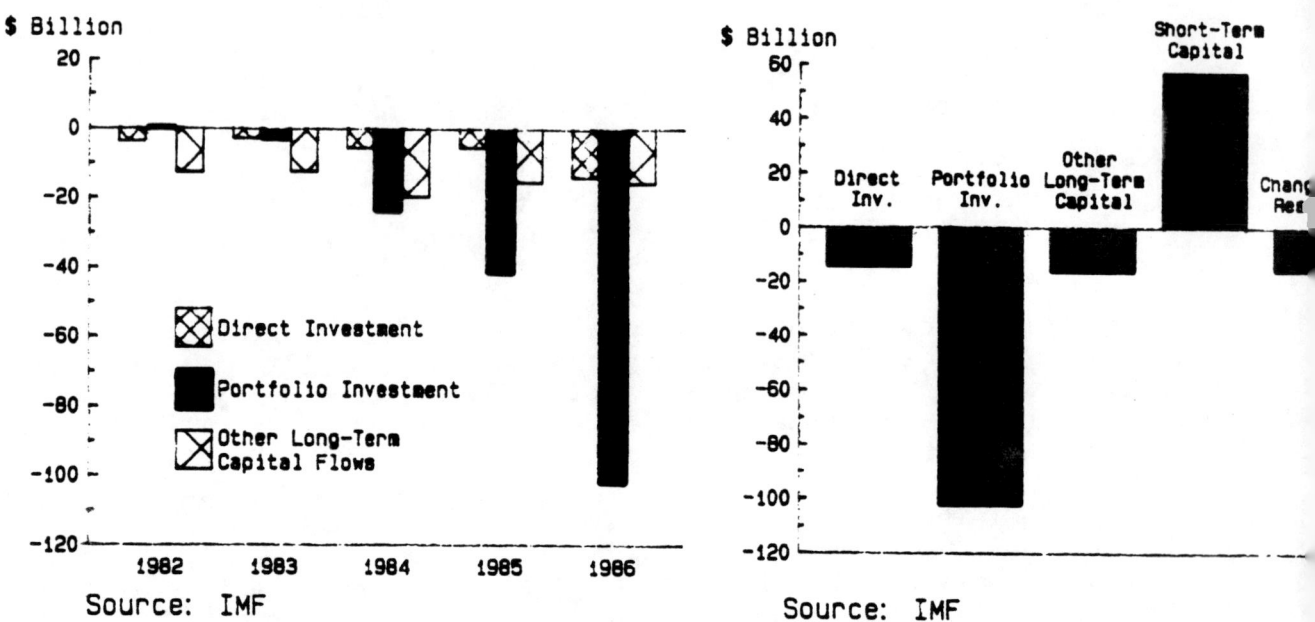

Figure 3
Japanese Net Long-Term Capital Flows 1982-1986
Source: IMF

Figure 4
Composition of Net Capital Flows 1986
Source: IMF

Because of yen appreciation, changes in the Japanese capital account appear greater in dollar terms than in yen terms. But whether measured dollars or yen, Japanese capital outflows have grown by substantial amounts. Furthermore, since Japan's current account is expected to remain in substantial surplus, capital outflows are likely to remain large.

LONG-TERM CAPITAL FLOWS

A clearer picture of trends in Japanese foreign investment is provided by a breakdown of long term capital flows (table 2).

The flow of long-term capital to Japan dropped sharply in 1986, while long-term capital outflows increased dramatically. There has little new foreign direct investment in Japan in recent years, and foreign portfolio investment in Japan in 1986 was limited to external bonds, which are issued in international markets by residents of Japan. These bonds, because of higher yields, have been more attractive to foreign investors than those issued in the Japanese domestic market. Foreigners were net sellers of Japanese equities in the past three years as price earning ratios of Japanese stocks had been two or three times higher than those of U.S. stocks and there had been an expectation of drop in the Japanese market well before the world-wide collapse of stock prices in October.

Table 2

Composition of Japan's Long-Term Capital Flows, 1982-86
(Billions of Dollars)

OUTFLOWS	1982	1983	1984	1985	1986
Securities	9.7	16.0	30.8	59.8	102.0
Bonds	6.1	12.5	26.8	53.5	93.0
Yen Bonds	3.5	2.9	4.0	5.3	1.9
Equities	0.2	0.7	0.1	1.0	7.0
Direct Investment	4.5	3.6	6.0	6.5	14.5
Loans Extended	7.9	8.4	11.9	10.4	9.3
Trade Credit	3.2	2.6	4.9	2.8	1.8
Other*	2.0	1.8	3.2	2.3	4.5
Total Long-Term Capital Outflows	27.4	32.5	56.8	81.8	132.1
INFLOWS					
Securities	11.9	14.1	7.2	16.7	0.5
External Bonds	4.3	5.7	7.4	12.9	18.4
Bonds	5.0	2.4	3.5	4.5	-2.1
Equities	2.5	6.1	-3.6	-0.7	-15.8
Direct Investment	0.4	0.4	0	0.6	0.2
Loans Received	-0.2	0	-0.1	-0.1	0
Trade Credit	0	0	0	0	0
Other	0.3	0.2	0	-0.1	-0.1
Total Long-Term Capital Inflows	12.4	14.8	7.1	17.3	0.6

Source: Bank of Japan, <u>Balance of Payments Monthly</u>

Portfolio Investment

The largest component of Japan's capital exports is portfolio investment, which includes bonds and ownership less than 10 percent of a company's stock. Bond purchases have increased about 15-fold since 1982, and accounted for 91 percent of portfolio investments made in 1986, up from 62 percent in 1982.

-The rate of return on foreign securities, even taking into account exchange rate effects, has generally been higher than on Japanese securities.

---

*includes such items as liabilities constituting foreign authorities' reserves. For more detail, see the IMF <u>Balance of Payments Manual</u>.

-The government has encouraged private capital outflows as a means of slowing the appreciation of the yen through financial liberalization, raising the ceiling on purchases of foreign securities by insurance companies and trust banks from 10 to 30 percent of their assets.

Overseas Direct Investment

Capital outflows attributed to direct investment abroad were 22 percent higher in 1986 than in 1982.

-The strong yen has caused producers to shift production facilities abroad in order to remain competitive.

-Foreign acquisitions have become cheaper and therefore more attractive to Japanese investors as a result of the appreciation of the yen since 1985.

-Threats of protectionist actions overseas lend added impetus to the move to locate production facilities abroad as Japanese producers attempt to protect their foreign markets.

In 1986, Japanese direct investment continued to climb, increasing in every region of the world except the Middle East (table 3).

-North America, primarily the United States, was the recipient of 45 percent of total Japanese direct investment in 1986, up from 35 percent in 1982. Seventy-five percent of the $10.2 billion invested in 1986 was in the commerce and service sector, including $3.7 billion in real estate (tables 4 and 5).

-Europe took $3.5 billion or 15.5 percent of total direct investment in FY 1986. Sixty-six percent of this was in financial institutions (banking, finance and insurance).

-The flow of direct investment to Latin America almost doubled from 1985 to 1986. The banking and insurance sectors in Panama, the Cayman Islands and the Bahamas attracted almost 5 percent of 1986 direct investment in Latin America as the Japanese developed institutions through which they could take advantage of low levels of taxation and lax capital controls in these countries. The transportation sector received $1.5 billion in 1986, most of this going to Panama which is an international shipping center because of the canal.

Table 3

Japanese Overseas Direct Investment[1] Flows by Country, FY[2] 1982-86
(Millions of Dollars)[3]

	FY 1982	FY 1983	FY 1984	FY 1985	FY 1986
United States	2738	2565	3360	5395	10165
Canada	167	136	184	100	276
North America	2905	2701	3544	5495	10441
Panama	722	1223	1671	1533	2401
Caymans	6	1	1	132	930
Bahamas	0	1	97	298	792
Brazil	322	410	318	314	270
Mexico	143	121	56	101	226
Bermuda	5	14	29	148	16
Peru	185	0	6	10	0
Latin America	1503	1878	2290	2616	4737
Hong Kong	400	563	412	131	502
Korea	103	129	107	134	436
Singapore	180	322	225	339	302
Taiwan	55	103	65	114	291
Indonesia	410	374	374	408	250
China	0	0	114	110	226
Malaysia	83	140	142	79	158
Thailand	94	72	119	48	124
Philippines	34	65	46	61	21
Asia	1384	1847	1628	1435	2327
Kuwait	41	66	55	34	41
Iran	0	1	0	0	0
Middle East	124	175	273	45	44
Luxembourg	127	265	315	300	1092
United Kingdom	176	153	318	375	984
Netherlands	73	113	452	613	651
West Germany	194	117	245	172	210
France	102	93	117	67	152
Switzerland	79	37	229	60	91
Spain	19	52	140	91	86
Belgium	64	126	71	84	50
Europe	876	990	1937	1930	3469
Liberia	434	323	281	159	289
Africa	489	364	326	172	309
Australia	370	166	105	468	881
Oceania	421	191	157	525	992
Total	7703	8145	10155	12217	22319

Source: JEI Report NO 25B, from Ministry of Finance

1/Direct investment data provided by the Ministry of Finance consists of investments of which the Ministry has been notified. Since there is a time lag between notification and implementation, these figures do not represent actual outflows of capital in the fiscal year.

2/The Japanese fiscal year begins April 1.

3/Japanese direct investment figures were published in dollar terms by the Ministry of Finance, which did not release exchange rate used.

4/Japanese data do not include reinvested earnings. However, U.S. data indicate that reinvested earnings from Japanese investment in the United States totalled less than $1 billion annually in 1982-1986.

-In 1986, one-third of the $2.3 billion direct investment in Asia was in production facilities, especially electronics. The East Asian NICs took 65 percent of Japanese direct investment in Asia in 1986, up from 50 percent in 1985, with the flow of direct investment to both Korea and Hong Kong increasing more than 200 percent.

Table 4

Japanese Overseas Direct Investment by Sector and Region, FY 1986
(Millions of Dollars)*

	Mfg	Natural Resources	Commerce & Services**	Branch Offices	Tot
North America	2198	136	7818	289	104
Latin America	272	114	4348	1	47
Asia	803	247	1213	66	23
Middle East	0	0	0	42	
Europe	369	27	2903	167	34
Africa	7	12	288	0	3
Oceania	150	202	646	0	9
Total	3800	737	17217	565	223

Source: UBS-Phillips & Drew, "Tsunami Alert," 7 August 1987
From Ministry of Finance and JEXIM Bank

Japanese direct investment in every region of the world was dominated by the commerce and service sector. Financial sector investments were significant, especially in Europe, Latin America and North America, while real estate was a large portion of investments only in North America. The transportation sector was relatively important in Latin America and Africa.

---

*The data in Tables 4 and 5 were computed from UBS-Phillips & Drew data that listed sectoral investment as percentage of total investment. Therefore, the figures in Tables 4 and 5 differ slightly from the data in Table 3.

**Commerce and Services includes the real estate sector.

Table 5

Japanese Overseas Direct Investment in Commerce and Services, FY 1986
(Millions of Dollars)

	Commerce	Finance & Insurance	Transportation	Real Estate	Other	Total
North America	1048	2056	27	3681	1006	7818
Latin America	130	2520	1548	4	147	4349
Asia	210	290	6	96	611	1213
Middle East	0	0	0	0	0	
Europe	387	2281	10	88	138	2904
Africa	0	0	285	0	3	288
Oceania	84	94	52	132	284	646
Total	1859	7240	1927	4001	2190	17217

Source: UBS-Phillips & Drew

COMPARISON OF JAPANESE CAPITAL FLOWS TO THOSE OF OTHER INDUSTRIAL NATIONS

Much attention has recently been focused on Japan and its growing holdings abroad. Japanese overseas direct investment has been growing at an increasingly rapid rate. However, its direct investment holdings are still dwarfed by those of the United States and the United Kingdom (table 6). When measured in terms of per capita holdings or as a percentage of GNP, Japanese overseas direct investment is at a much lower level than that of other industrial nations (figures 5 and 6).

Table 6

Stock of Overseas Direct Investments: Selected Countries
(Billions of Dollars)

	end of year 1984	1985	1986	% change 1984-1985	1985-86
United States	213.0	232.7	259.9	9.25	11.69
U.K.	100.6	116.9	133.9	16.20	14.54
Japan	37.9	44.0	58.1	16.09	32.05
West Germany	36.6	52.4	n/a	43.17	n/a
Canada	31.6	33.5	n/a	6.01	n/a
Netherlands	40.5	55.5	n/a	37.04	n/a

Sources: "JETRO White Paper on World and Japanese Overseas and Direct Investment," Survey of Current Business, Japanese Balance of Payments Monthly, and The United Kingdom's Balance of Payments.

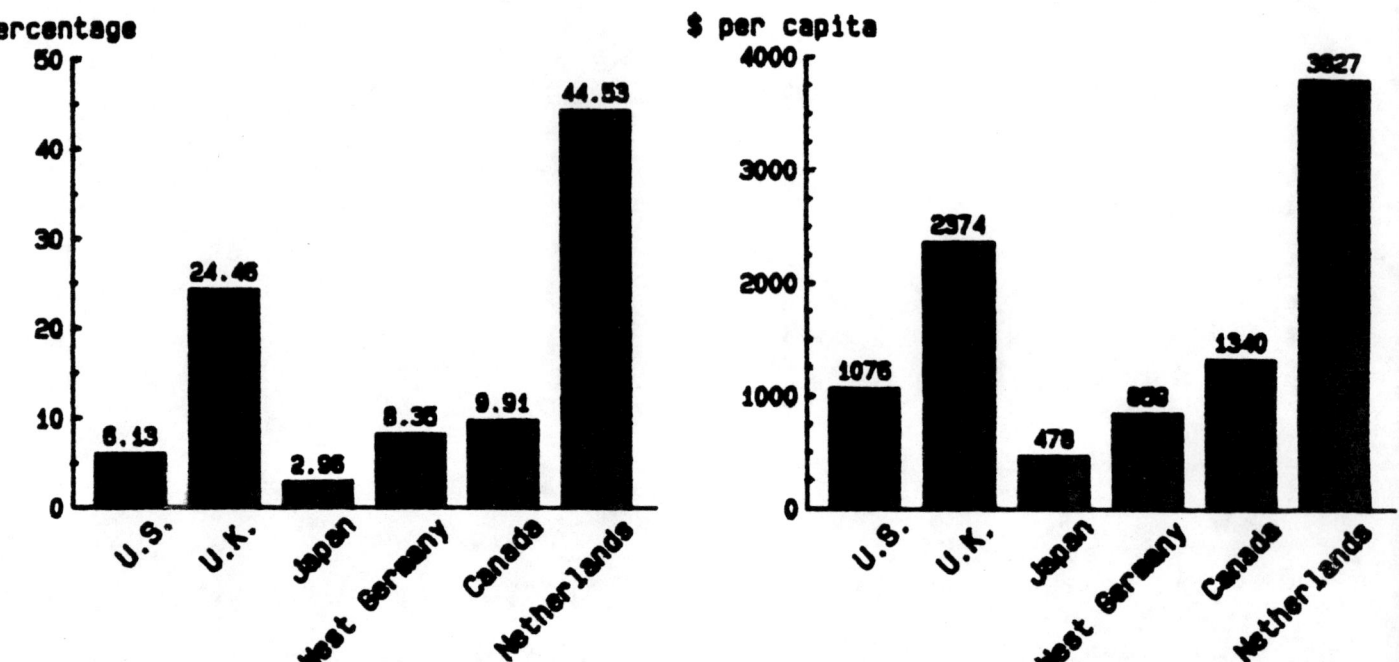

Figure 5

Overseas Direct Investment as Percentage of GNP end of year, 1985 or 1986*

Figure 6

Overseas Direct Investment per Capita end of year, 1985 or 1986*

*For the U.S., U.K. and Japan, 1986 data are used. 1985 data are used for West Germany, Canada and the Netherlands.

Source: Drawn from IMF and Morgan Guaranty Data and figures in Table

Although both West Germany and Japan are running large current account surpluses, West Germany, unlike Japan, is a net importer of long term capital. In 1986, foreigners' purchases of German bonds rose to almost $27 billion, up almost 87 percent above the previous year's purchases. Also in contrast with Japan, Germany has had a substantial outflow of short-term capital, reflecting the fact that Germany's interest rates are among the lowest in Europe. The counterparts of the large current account surplus and long-term capital inflows have been short-term capital outflows.

THE CONCENTRATION OF JAPANESE INVESTMENT IN THE UNITED STATES

Japanese direct and portfolio investment is concentrated in the United States (table 7). Portfolio investment has been attracted to the U.S. by higher rates of return in spite of exchange rate uncertainties and the depth of the U.S. market as well as by the economic stability and market potential which draw direct investment. Moreover, since 198 investment in the United States has gained more appeal because of the strengthened yen.

Table 7

Japanese Long-Term Net Capital Outflows by Region, 1986
(Millions of Dollars)

	U.S.	E.C.	Other Countries	Other*	Total
Direct Investment	7774	2694	378	0	14254
Trade Credits	334	1087	455	0	1876
Loans	690	1038	8215	-628	9315
Securities	55944	29013	12667	3808	101432
Other	908	554	642	2480	4584
Total	65650	34386	25765	5660	131461

*multilateral institutions and unallocated flows
Source: JEI Report NO. 29B, from Bank of Japan

JAPANESE CAPITAL FLOWS IN FIRST HALF OF 1987

Large and increasing Japanese purchases of foreign securities continued into the first half of 1987. Bond purchases remained strong, with a slight shift away from U.S. bonds in favor of West German and other bonds. Net purchases of foreign stocks increased at a annual rate 2.8 times the 1986 level. Data from the Japan Securities Dealers Association indicate that stock purchases were concentrated in the United States, especially in the first quarter 1987. In the second quarter, stock purchases were more diverse, with a rising share going to the United Kingdom and other countries. In the third quarter of 1987, purchases of foreign securities declined, suggesting that Japanese capital exports may have peaked.

It is difficult to ascertain the effect of the recent stock market turmoil on Japanese long-term portfolio investment abroad. In October, the Japanese were net sellers of foreign bonds. But even before the stock market fell, Japanese purchases of foreign bonds had slowed, reflecting expectations of a rise in U.S. interest rates and further appreciation of the yen. Since the October 19 fall of global stock markets, Japanese purchases of foreign equities have dropped. However, Japanese investors were net purchasers of foreign equities in October, indicating that they did not pull out of the market on a large scale. In regard to future foreign portfolio investments, the Japanese appear to be waiting for clearer signs as to future movements in the U.S. budget and trade deficits. Nevertheless, as long as the Japanese remain in current account surplus--as is expected--they must by definition remain capital exporters.

PART TWO: THE ROLE OF JAPANESE CAPITAL EXPORTS IN LDCs

In recent years, net financial flows from developed to developing nations have decreased. Japan, with its huge current account surpluses, is in a position to export substantial amounts of capital to LDCs and thus ease financial strains and promote development in debtor countries. Thus, Japan has been coming under increasing pressures to recycle much more of its huge capital surpluses to developing and debtor nations.

THE FLOW OF FINANCIAL RESOURCES TO DEVELOPING COUNTRIES

Net private capital flows from developed to developing nations dropped from a peak of $74.3 billion in 1981 to $29.4 billion in 1985, and export credits decreased by 16.8 billion to $1.2 billion. With private flows declining as a percentage of total flows, official development assistance (ODA) has become more important. Private capital flows from Japan, however, have not followed a downward trend. According to OECD figures, net financial flows from Japan to developing nations increased 28% between 1982 and 1985, from $8.7 billion to $11.2 billion, with private capital flows becoming more important and official flows decreasing as a percentage of the total (figure 7). Japanese statistics indicate that in 1986, net long-term capital flows were at least $20 billion.

Figure 7

Flow of Financial Resources to Developing Countries from Japan and DAC* countries

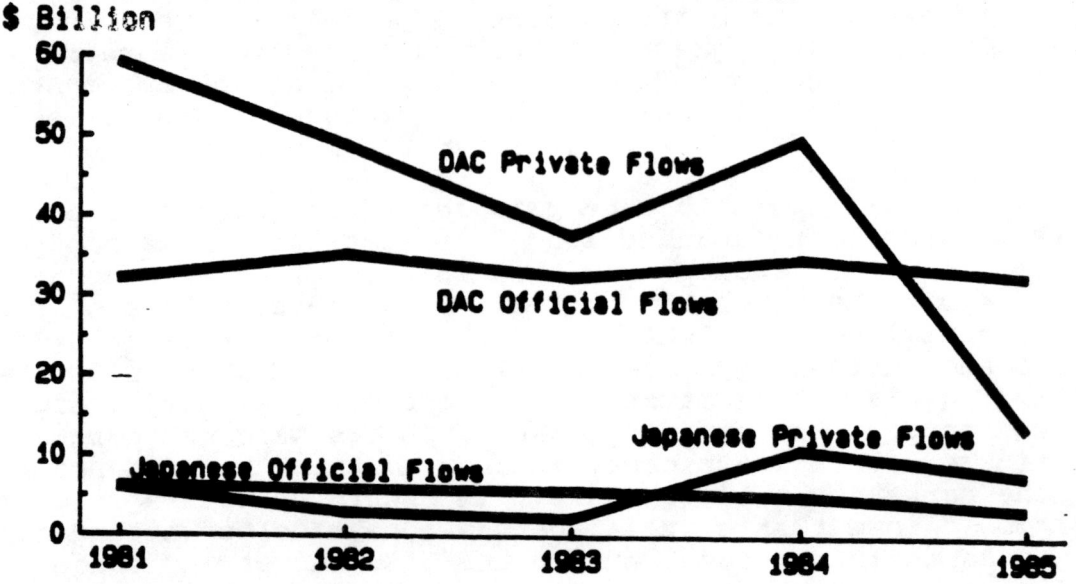

Source: OECD, Development Cooperation, 1986 Report

*Development Assistance Committee: membership includes most of the countries in the Organization of Economic Cooperation and Development (OECD)

The Role of Japanese Private Sector Capital

According to OECD data, capital flows from Japan's private sector accounted for about 38 percent of all private flows to the developing nations from DAC countries in 1985. Investment in securities of multilateral lending institutions accounted for about 60 percent of Japanese private capital flows, and direct investment accounted for 12 percent.

Japanese banks, like their western counterparts, have been reluctant to continue lending to countries with debt servicing difficulties. At the same time, demand for commercial bank financing by the more creditworthy developing nations--most are in Asia--has decreased. Bond lending--mostly to a few Asian and European nations and financed increasingly by the Japanese--is growing. In 1986, Japan became the prime source of funds for LDC borrowers.

In the past several years, Japanese direct investment in developing countries has been largely in Asia and Latin America. Investment in Latin America has primarily been in the financial sector and, to a lesser extent, in the transportation sector, while investment in Asia has been in manufacturing as well as commerce and services (see tables 3, 4 and 5).

The Role of Japanese Government Capital

Japanese government capital (table 8) enters developing country economies primarily in two ways: through ODA including subscriptions to multilateral lending agencies, and through official export credits.

Table 8

Official Japanese Financial Flows to Developing Countries and Multilateral Lending Agencies, 1982-86
(Millions of Dollars)

	1982	1983	1984	1985	1986
Official Development Assistance	$3,023	$3,761	$4,319	$3,797	$5,634
Bilateral Assistance	2,367	2,425	2,427	2,557	3,846
Grants	805	993	1,064	1,185	1,703
Capital Grant Assistance	412	535	543	636	855
Technical Assistance	393	458	521	549	849
Development Lending and Capital	1,562	1,432	1,363	1,372	2,143
Multilateral Subscriptions, Grants and Loans	656	1,336	1,891	1,240	1,788
Other Official Flows	2791	1954	743	-302	n/a
Bilateral	1136	2821	1914	873	n/a
Multilateral	-31	41	-130	-148	n/a

Source: JEI Report, NO. 22B, from Ministry of Foreign Affairs

A large portion of ODA has gone to Asian countries, although the Japanese government has stated that it will diversify future disbursements of aid. Japanese ODA in dollar terms increased substantially in 1986, although most of the increase can be attribu to exchange rate movements.

The Japanese government has pledged to double its yearly commi to ODA by 1990 from its 1986 level of $5.6 billion. This does not necessarily indicate an increase in the amount of ODA funds going t debt-ridden countries, however. Government regulations restrict disbursement of these funds to countries with a per capita income b $2000, and countries which are in arrears are ineligible for new lo In line with the market orientation of the Japanese government, ODA contingent upon the adoption of an IMF standby program which genera requires structural adjustment and market oriented reforms by the recipient.

Net Japanese official export credits to developing nations were negative in 1985, meaning that repayments exceeded new loans made.

JAPANESE POSITION ON THE DEBT CRISIS

With a developing country debt exposure second only to that of United States (table 9), Japan has a strong interest in resolving t debt crisis. The official Japanese position stresses the need for market-oriented solutions. The Japanese government officially suppo the Baker initiative and is critical of any plan which involves debt forgiveness. Debtor countries are expected to implement structural adjustment policies in order to attract foreign investors and incre international trade.

Table 9

Exposure of Japanese and U.S. Commercial Banks to Selected Natio
End of Year, 1985
(Billions of Dollars)

	Total, all Commercial Banks	Japanese Banks Amount	% of Total	U.S. Banks Amount	% of Tot
Mexico	76.1	12.9	17.0	24.4	32.1
Brazil	80.0	10.7	13.4	23.6	29.5
Argentina	32.9	5.4	16.4	8.7	26.4
Venezuela	28.9	4.4	15.3	9.8	33.9
Philippines	14.5	2.7	18.8	5.1	35.2
Chile	14.3	1.7	11.8	6.2	43.4
Ecuador	5.2	0.9	16.7	2.0	38.5
Yugoslavia	10.5	0.8	7.4	2.2	21.0
Poland	10.0	0.6	6.3	0.5	5.0

Sources: Morgan International Data and estimates from Japan Economic Journal, June 6, 1987

Under pressure from the government, Japanese banks participated in the first major lending operation attributed to the Baker initiative in which $7.7 billion in loans was extended to Mexico by commercial banks. Japanese banks, like their U.S. counterparts, are reluctant to continue lending to indebted nations. One concession which Japanese banks were seeking was more generous tax treatment of banks' reserves against bad loans. Although the government has not acquiesced on this point, it has allowed the creation of a "paper company" in the Cayman Islands to which Japanese Banks can sell non-performing loans at a discount which is fully tax-deductible. As shareholders in the company, the participating banks receive dividends when payments are made on outstanding loans.

RECENT INITIATIVES BY THE JAPANESE GOVERNMENT

In response to growing pressures, primarily from the United States but also from the rest of the developed and developing world, the Japanese government has announced a plan to recycle a portion of its current account surpluses to the developing world through fiscal year 1990. The plan was designed in part to stem criticism that the Japanese were not meeting their responsibility to finance needy nations, a responsibility dictated by their position as the world's number one capital exporter. Probably by no coincidence, the plan was announced during Prime Minister Nakasone's visit to Washington in April 1986.

The details of this plan remain unclear. It is referred to by some as a $20 billion recycling plan and by others as a $30 billion plan, the $10 billion difference being money that was pledged to multilateral lending agencies prior to the announcement of the scheme.

The $10 billion previously pledged subscriptions represent most of the funds which will come directly from the government budget. These funds will go to the World Bank, the IMF and the Asian Development Bank, and represent annual subscriptions 80 percent over the amount pledged for 1987.

Except for loans made by the Overseas Economic Cooperation Fund (OECF), Japan's soft loan agency, the rest of the recycling plan calls for the disbursement of funds raised on the Japanese capital markets or provided by private banks. The government has been vague on details, but has provided a rough outline of the plan. Of the $20 billion additional money pledged, $8 billion will be made available to the multilateral development banks (MDBs) through increased access to Japanese capital markets, and $12 billion is to be lent by the Japanese Export-Import Bank (JEXIM), the OECF and private banks.

Of the $12 billion that is to be lent by JEXIM, OECF and private banks, about $9 billion is expected to be used in cofinancing World Bank loans. The OECF is expected to lend about $3 billion on concessional terms to IDA countries, those designated as the poorest of the developing nations by the World Bank.

The Impact of the Recycling Plan

It is difficult to judge the impact of the recycling plan at present time because the details are vague. It is likely that the will have a positive effect on capital flows to the developing nati although its impact will probably not be as great as appears at fir glance because much of the $30 billion seems to be a repackaging of programs and loans packages which would have existed in the absence comprehensive new recycling plan.

There are a number of developing countries which are able to b from commercial banks, and loans to these countries, which probably would be made in the absence in the recycling plan, will likely be classified as part of the plan. Incentives for additional lending indebted countries have not yet been announced. In the absence of measures, it is doubtful that there will be great amounts of new le to troubled debtors.

About a quarter of the funds in the recycling plan--$8 billion to be raised by the multilateral development banks (MDBs) on Japane capital markets. It is not clear, however, that the MDBs will be willing to raise that amount in three years. The MDBs are generall able to borrow as needed. Their lending is limited mainly by the s of their capital bases and their assessments of the amounts that prospective borrowers can effectively use. Thus, increased access Japanese capital markets will not necessarily add $8 billion to the amount that the MDBs will borrow in the next three years. Some por of what the MDBs borrow in Japan is likely to be in place of, and n addition to, borrowing elsewhere.

With respect to the $12 billion that Japan plans to lend direc to LDCs--rather than indirectly through MDBs--it is not clear what countries will be the recipients. The initiative appears to be dire primarily at middle income developing nations, those with "absorpti capacity." To be eligible to receive funds, a country must be in g standing with the World Bank, since its strict lending standards wi apply. Some observers believe that a major portion of these funds go to Latin America, while others believe the Japanese will follow traditional pattern by directing the majority of the funds to Asian nations.

THE FUTURE ROLE OF JAPANESE CAPITAL IN LDCs

Japanese capital exports to developing countries, though expec to remain a small portion of total Japanese capital outflows, are l to account for a sizable share of total developed country capital f to the third world. However, a large proportion of Japanese capita exports to the third world will probably continue to flow to Asian nations. As supporters of free market principles, the Japanese government is unlikely to take an interventionist role in the alloc of private sector capital.

And the private sector--left to its own devices--is likely to channel most of its investments in LDCs into relatively well-off Asian NICs and other financially healthy, growing LDC economies--where the risk is lower and the anticipated return higher than in troubled high-debt LDCs.

Official flows will probably be spread more widely over regional lines, especially given Japan's pledge to diversify its official development assistance. Asian nations, however--given Japan's strong economic and political interest in the region--are likely to continue to attract a significant portion of Japanese ODA. In sum, then, it is questionable that Japanese capital exports will contribute substantially to providing financial relief or promoting economic development in Latin American countries or countries elsewhere that are suffering from serious problems in servicing their external debt or whose prospects for economic development appear bleak.